100 AMAZING
RUGBY
FACTS

Interesting and Crazy RUGBY Stories and
Trivia for Smart Kids and Curious People

PRESENTATION

This book is part of the **WORLD STORIES ENCYCLOPEDIA series**, an important publishing project specialized in publications for children and teenagers, and suitable for curious people of all ages

Th series includes various books with a fascinating selection of **incredible stories, facts and curiosities about society, various sports, animals, nature, science.**

All achieved with the help and advice of **industry experts** to always provide high quality information and content.

The even more attractive thing is that through these books children and teenagers will perfect their cognitive and logical skills simply by having fun.
What's more beautiful?

Happy reading and have fun friends.

1

The Historical Origin of Rugby: A Game Born from an Improvised Gesture

Rugby, today a global sport, has its roots in a singular episode that occurred in 1823 in a rugby school in England. During a football match, a young student named William Webb Ellis did something unexpected: instead of playing according to the traditional rules of football, he grabbed the ball with his hands and ran towards the opponent's goal.

This act, considered rebellious and innovative for its time, marked the birth of rugby. That spontaneous and courageous moment is remembered as the spark that ignited interest in this sport, which has since gone through a path of continuous evolution, becoming a passion for millions of people around the world.

2

The Mystery of Numbers in Rugby: A Legacy of Roles and Functions

In rugby, each player on the field is identified by a number, which varies from 1 a15. These numbers are more than simple labels; they represent a historical tradition and the specific role of each player. For example, the number 2, assigned to the hooker, reflects his original responsibility to "hook" the ball in scrums.

Likewise, the number 10, worn by the fly-half or "fly-half", indicates his key position in the center of the pitch, orchestrating play and attacking strategies. This unique numbering not only defines the structure of the game but is also a tribute to its historical roots and the tactical evolution of rugby.

World Cup of Rugby: An Event That Unites the World

La Rugby World Cup is one of the most prestigious events in the international sporting scene. This tournament, which takes place every four years, is organized by World Rugby, and saw its first edition in 1987 in New Zealand and Australia. The victory of the New Zealand team that year marked the beginning of a new era in rugby.

The tournament is more than just a sporting competition; it is an event that celebrates international brotherhood, athletic excellence, and team spirit. Through la World Cup Rugby, nations from around the world come together, promoting not only the sport, but also the values of respect, unity, and shared passion for this dynamic and fascinating game.

4

The spirit of "Haka": Tradition and mental strength

One of the most iconic aspects of rugby is the "haka", a traditional Maori dance performed by the New Zealand national team, the All Blacks, before each match. This ancient ritual is an action of challenge and respect towards opponents.

The "haka" is a way to concentrate and mentally prepare players, as well as representing the pride of Maori culture in the context of international rugby; it is an experience full of symbolism and cultural pride, as well as becoming an icon of international rugby, commanding respect for the history and strength of the New Zealand team.

5

The value of sportsmanship: A gentleman's game

Rugby is known for its respect for the rules and the sporting spirit that permeates the playing field. Despite the intensity and physicality of the game, the players are known for their fair play and respect towards their opponents.

This value is emphasized by the tradition of exchanging jerseys at the end of a match, symbolizing mutual respect and friendship even after intense competition.

The British and Irish Lions: A Unique Rugby Institution

The British and Irish Lions team, a composite team drawn from England, Scotland, Wales, and Ireland, represents a unique tradition in rugby union. Established in 1888, the Lions tour to the Southern Hemisphere to play against New Zealand, Australia, and South Africa, usually every four years. These tours are renowned for their spirit of camaraderie, sportsmanship, and the immense challenge they pose, given the strength of the Southern Hemisphere teams.

The Lions tours are a significant highlight in the rugby calendar, creating some of the most memorable moments in the sport's history. The concept of the Lions transcends national rivalries within the British Isles, promoting a sense of unity and collective pride. The selection of players is a prestigious honor, reflecting the highest level of achievement and recognition in British and Irish rugby.

7

The Twickenham Stadium: More Than Just a Venue

Twickenham Stadium, located in southwest London, is the largest stadium in the world dedicated solely to rugby union. It is affectionately known as the "Home of England Rugby" and has a capacity of 82,000 spectators. The stadium's history dates back to 1907 when the land was purchased by the Rugby Football Union to develop a dedicated rugby venue. Twickenham has since evolved into a cultural icon within the sport, hosting its first international match in 1910 between England and Wales. Beyond its role as a sports venue, Twickenham has a deep emotional resonance within the rugby community, embodying the sport's traditions, history, and values.

The stadium also houses the World Rugby Museum, which offers insights into the global impact of rugby, celebrating its heritage and the legendary figures who have graced the sport.

8

Rugby Sevens and Global Outreach

Rugby sevens, a variant of rugby union with teams made up of seven players playing seven-minute halves, was invented in Melrose, Scotland, in 1883 but has become a significant part of British rugby's contribution to the global game. The faster-paced, more open game format has gained popularity worldwide, leading to its inclusion in the Olympic Games starting in 2016. British teams, particularly those from England and Scotland, have been instrumental in the development and success of rugby sevens, contributing to its innovative tactics and thrilling gameplay.

The inclusion of rugby sevens in the Olympics marks a significant milestone in rugby's history, showcasing the sport's adaptability and appeal to a global audience. This adaptation not only highlights the dynamic nature of rugby but also its ability to evolve and captivate new fans across the world, reinforcing its status as a truly international sport.

The Calcutta Cup: A Trophy With Unique Origins

The Calcutta Cup is one of rugby's oldest and most prestigious trophies, contested annually by England and Scotland as part of the Six Nations Championship. Its origins, however, are deeply rooted in the history of rugby in India. In 1872, a group of rugby enthusiasts in Calcutta (now Kolkata) formed the Calcutta Football Club. The club faced difficulties due to the tropical climate and a lack of interest, leading to its dissolution in 1878. The remaining club members decided to withdraw the club's funds, which had been held in silver rupees, and melt them down into a trophy to be presented to the Rugby Football Union (RFU) with the request that it be competed for in a manner that would best promote the interests of rugby. The Calcutta Cup was made from 270 silver rupees and first competed for in 1879. It embodies the global reach and historical depth of rugby, connecting the sport's present to its past in unexpected ways.

10

The strength of solidarity: The rugby community

Rugby is more than a sport; it's a community. Players, fans, and coaches form a strong bond that goes beyond the playing field. Commitment to rugby teaches the importance of teamwork, loyalty, and solidarity. Many players dedicate their time to volunteering to promote the game among young people and to support social causes, creating a lasting bond between people of different backgrounds and cultures.

11

Rugby as a tool for inclusion and diversity

Rugby is open to everyone, regardless of size, physical shape, or cultural background. It is a sport that celebrates diversity and promotes inclusion. There are special teams and programs designed to involve players with disabilities, giving everyone the opportunity to actively participate and enjoy the benefits that sport can offer. This inclusiveness is a fundamental pillar of modern rugby.

12

The mysterious rules: The complexity and logic of the regulation

Rugby is known for its regulatory complexity, with rules that can appear confusing to those unfamiliar with the game. However, these rules have their own logic and are designed to ensure safety, fairness and spectacularity.

For example, the concept of "advantage" allows the game to continue even after a rule violation, as long as the offending team is not at a disadvantage, thus keeping the game fluid and exciting.

13

The global growth of rugby

Rugby, once concentrated primarily in nations such as the United Kingdom, Francia, Australia, and New Zealand, is experiencing exponential growth globally, even in countries not traditionally associated with the sport.

This global growth is the result of strategic investments, with a particular focus on youth training, increased television coverage and the introduction of international tournaments and professional competitions.

Rugby's expansion beyond its traditional boundaries is helping not only diversify the sporting landscape, but also create a more inclusive and global environment for this exciting sport.

14

The legacy of rugby

Rugby is more than just a sport; represents a rich cultural tradition and legacy that is passed down from generation to generation. This sport has deep roots in many nations, where it is more than a competition: it is a central element of national and cultural identity.

The fundamental values of rugby, such as respect, integrity, and solidarity, are taught from an early age and are considered an integral part of sports education. These values, combined with the physical and strategic nature of the game, make rugby one of a kind. Rugby fans and players are not just spectators or athletes; they are custodians of a heritage that continues to evolve while maintaining its roots.

15

Record in the world of rugby

Dan Carter, a New Zealand rugby legend, holds the record for most points scored in an international career, with over 1,500 points. His career was dotted with extraordinary moments, which made him one of the best openers in the history of rugby.

His ability to play with his foot, his precision in conversions and set pieces, and his vision of the game have left an indelible mark on the panorama of world rugby. His legacy goes beyond records: Carter was a role model of play and sportsmanship, inspiring generations of players around the world.

16

Rules of the game

The 'Drop Goal': The 'Drop Goal' is one of the different ways in which points can be scored in rugby. Unlike the 'Try' and 'Conversions', the 'Drop Goal' can be made at any point in the game, and is often a strategic weapon at critical moments of the match. To score a 'Drop Goal', the player must bounce the ball on the ground before hitting it with his foot, trying to pass it over the crossbar and between the opposing posts.

This technique requires skill, timing, and precision, and can be decisive, especially in balanced matches where every point is fundamental. 'Drop Goals' are celebrated for their difficulty and the emotion they can generate, especially when scored in the dying moments of a match.

17

Wacky curiosities

The longest match: In 2015, in Norway, one of the longest rugby matches in history took place, lasting 42 consecutive hours. This event not only set a world record for duration, but also served a charitable purpose, raising funds for various charitable causes.

The match attracted attention not only for its unusual length, but also because it highlighted rugby in a region where it has traditionally not been a very popular sport. This extraordinary event demonstrated rugby's ability to bring people together for a common cause, and helped spread interest in the sport to a new geographic area.

18

Unusual rules

The "unexpected" ball: In rugby, there is a particular rule regarding situations in which the ball leaves the field of play and hits an unexpected external object, such as a billboard or a foreign object. In such cases, the referee stops the game and awards a throw of the ball to the team that did not cause the outing.

This rule was introduced to keep the game fair and predictable, preventing external factors from influencing the outcome of a match. It is an example of how rugby, despite being a sport with a long history, continues to evolve and adapt to ensure the best possible playing experience.

19

Impressive records

Most successful team: The New Zealand All Blacks are known in the rugby world for their extraordinary win rate. With a percentage hovering around 80%, this team has established one of the most impressive records in the world of sports. Their history is characterized by success in both international competitions and test matches, demonstrating a consistency and quality of play that few other teams can claim.

The All Blacks are a symbol of excellence in rugby, known for their intensity, their tactical and physical prowess, and for the famous 'Haka', a Maori dance performed before each match, which has become an icon of rugby in world level.

20

Intriguing rules

The "Sin Bin": The "Sin Bin" is a disciplinary sanction used in rugby to manage offenses of a certain severity. When a player commits a foul considered serious, but not enough to justify a permanent expulsion, he is sent to the "Sin Bin" for a period of 10 minutes.

During this time, the penalized player's team must play outnumbered, facing a significant challenge. This rule was introduced to emphasize the importance of fair play and discipline on the pitch. The "Sin Bin" also serves as a deterrent against bad behaviour, maintaining the integrity of the sport.

21

Unique curiosities

The record for the longest kick: Ollie Phillips, a former professional 15s and 7s rugby player, holds the record for the longest kick in rugby. During a promotional event, Phillips delivered an impressive kick of 77 meters, demonstrating extraordinary power and precision.

This record highlights not only Phillips' individual ability but also the potential physical reach that rugby players can achieve. These spectacular moments help elevate the image of rugby, showcasing the level of skill and strength that the game requires.

22

The world record for the longest rugby match
In 2017, in South Africa, a rugby match took place that broke all previous records for its duration, stretching for 28 hours without interruption. This rugby marathon tested the physical and mental endurance of the players in a way never seen before.

In addition to the athletic aspect, the match also had a strong social and charitable impact, with the aim of raising funds for various charitable causes. The event attracted global attention, not only for its gruelling nature but also for its spirit of community and solidarity, reflecting rugby's unique ability to bring people together for noble causes.

23

Record attendance: Full stadiums

Soweto Stadium, also known as FNB Stadium or Soccer City, is a monument in the world of rugby. With an impressive capacity of over 94,000 spectators, it is the largest stadium dedicated exclusively to rugby. As well as hosting the Rugby World Cup final in 1995, it has witnessed numerous other historic events.

Its grandeur and its ability to bring so many people together for sport represents not only the popularity of rugby in South Africa, but also the stadium's role as a symbol of unity and national pride.

24

Rules of respect: "Silence" during kicks

One of the most notable traditions in rugby is the practice of silence by the public during kick attempts. This rule of conduct, unique in the world of sport, emphasizes respect for the player and the integrity of the game.

In these moments of silence, the atmosphere in the stadium becomes full of tension and anticipation, with the entire crowd awaiting the football result. This practice deeply reflects the core values of rugby: respect, honour, and fair play.

25

Record attendance on the pitch

Richie McCaw, with 148 international matches under his belt, is not only an icon of New Zealand rugby but also a symbol of endurance and longevity in the sport. His career, filled with high-level performances, displays a rare combination of physical ability, tactical intelligence, and leadership.

His presence on the field was a point of reference and a role model for rugby players around the world, setting a high standard for future generations.

26

Wacky Curiosities: The "L'homme Volant"

The 1977 event, when Henri Durand unexpectedly parachuted onto the pitch during a rugby match between France and Wales, has gone down in legend. This spectacular performance, both daring and humorous, captured the imagination of audiences worldwide.

Not only did it add an element of surprise and fun to that game, but it also highlighted how rugby can be a platform for unique and memorable expressions.

27

The record of tries scored

Joe Rokocoko's record of four tries scored in a single international match against Italy in 2003 demonstrates his exceptional talent as a fullback. His ability to read the game, exploit opportunities and display extraordinary speed and agility on the pitch has made him one of the most feared and respected forwards in world rugby.

28

Curiosities about mixes: The "spoon"

The "spoon" technique in the scrum is a demonstration of the tactical complexity and ingenuity in rugby. This move, which requires high skill and precision, allows the hooker to manipulate the ball more effectively and unpredictably, giving his team a strategic advantage. The presence of such techniques highlights the depth and variety of the game of rugby, combining physical ability and tactical ingenuity.

29

The World Cup Epic: The Underdog Challenge

Japan's victory against South Africa in 2015 at Rugby World Cup was a moment of great historical significance in the world of rugby. Japanese National Team, considered by many to be an "underdog" in that competition, amazed the whole world.

South Africa, holders of two world titles, were clear favourites against Japan. However, the Brave Blossoms, led by their coach Eddie Jones, showed unparalleled determination. This victory not only strengthened the prestige of Japanese rugby, but also demonstrated that in rugby, as in many other sports, nothing is guaranteed and inertia can change in an instant.

30

Speed record: The fastest football

The record for the fastest kick recorded in a rugby match belongs to Welsh rugby legend Neil Jenkins. Jenkins scored a kick at an estimated rate of about 108 miles per hour, equivalent to approximately 174 kilometres per hour. This incredible kick was performed during a match, demonstrating Jenkins' extraordinary power and accuracy.

The moment when a kicker of such caliber executes such a powerful kick is always impressive, but this record underlined Jenkins' extraordinary strength and technical ability as one of the best half-stops in rugby history.

31

Curiosities about humanitarian initiatives: The "highest match"

In 2005, a unique event took place on the slopes of Everest, where a rugby match was played at an extraordinary altitude of more than 6.000 meters. This event, in addition to setting a record for the highest altitude rugby match, was intended to raise funds for humanitarian initiatives.

The players, facing extreme conditions and an unprecedented physical challenge, demonstrated incredible team spirit and resilience. This feat also attracted global attention for the humanitarian cause supported, highlighting how rugby can be a vehicle for positive social change and raising awareness of global issues.

32

The concept of "transformation"

After scoring a try, rugby offers the opportunity for a "transformation". This kick attempt, which aims to pass the ball between the posts, is worth an additional two points. Transformation requires a combination of precision, power, and mental stability, often performed under pressure and in variable conditions.

The ability to successfully convert a try can be crucial to the outcome of a match, demonstrating the importance of kicking technique in modern rugby.

33

Curiosities about the playing fields: The Millennium Stadium

The Millennium Stadium in Cardiff, with its retractable roof, is a marvel of modern engineering. This feature allows you to play in ideal conditions regardless of the weather, creating a unique atmosphere for players and spectators.

The innovative roof design not only protects the pitch and the audience from the elements, but also allows it to host a variety of events, making the stadium a multi-purpose landmark in the sporting and cultural landscape.

34

The meaning of nicknames: The "All Blacks"

The nickname "All Blacks" of the New Zealand national rugby team has now become synonymous with excellence in sport. The name comes from the all-black colour of their uniforms, but the meaning goes far beyond the visual aspect.

The All Blacks embody values of strength, skill, and a rugby culture that emphasizes teamwork, resilience, and intensity. Their presence on the field is a symbol of a rich and respected sporting tradition, which inspires millions of fans around the world.

35

The importance of the team captain

In rugby, the captain plays a crucial role that transcends simple leadership and representation functions. He is the central figure in game strategy, communication with the referee, and team motivation. The captain must possess not only physical and technical skills, but also tactical intelligence and leadership ability that can significantly influence the outcome of a match. It is the fulcrum around which team spirit and collective identity are built.

The evolution of protective equipment

In the history of rugby, protective equipment has undergone a radical transformation. Originally, players wore simple, minimal clothing, but as the intensity and physicality of the game increased, so did the need for better protection.

Today, equipment includes ergonomic helmets, shoulder pads, shin guards and gloves, all designed to absorb impacts and reduce the risk of injury. This evolution reflects the importance placed on player safety in contemporary rugby, balancing the need for protection with maintaining the fluidity and dynamism of the game.

37

The "TMO" (Television Match Official) protocol

TMO is a protocol used in rugby refereeing that allows referees to request video assistance to make decisions on doubtful or unclear situations, such as confirming the validity of a try, verifying a foul or analysing any irregular game situations not observed initially. This tool aims to improve the correctness of referee decisions during the match.

38

Game ethics and respect towards the referee
One of the distinctive characteristics of rugby is the importance placed on respect towards the referee. Players are educated from a young age to respect the referee's decisions, to avoid unsportsmanlike behaviour and to maintain a respectful attitude even in the tensest situations. This value is part of the ethics of the game and helps maintain fair play on the pitch.

39

World record for most points scored in a rugby match

The world record for the most points scored in an international rugby match was set in 2002. During a match between Namibia and Sierra Leone during the 2003 Rugby World Cup qualifiers, Namibia triumphed by scoring 188 points against 6 of Sierra Leone.

This result represents one of the largest scoring discrepancies ever recorded in an international rugby match. The incredible scoring disparity highlighted the huge differences in level between the two teams, highlighting the competitive asymmetry between nations with different degrees of experience, development, and investment in the sport.

The key role of coaches

Coaches in rugby play a crucial role in the development of teams. In addition to managing the technical and tactical aspects, they are responsible for creating a cohesive environment, developing players' individual skills, and forging a winning mentality. A good coach not only imparts technical knowledge, but is also a leader, motivator and mentor who guides players towards success.

41

Jonah Lomu's rugby story

Jonah Lomu was one of the most iconic and influential players in rugby history. Of New Zealand origin, Lomu was an undisputed rugby legend, famous for his physical power, speed, and ability to break through opposing defences.

His notoriety peaked during the South Africa la Rugby World Cup 1995, in, where Lomu emerged as a dominant force, crushing opponents with his unstoppable power. He was one of the first players to achieve global fame in rugby, and his untimely death due 2015 to complications from kidney disease made him an even more legendary figure in the world of sport.

42

The evolution of game strategy

Rugby has undergone a notable evolution in game strategies over the years. We have moved from a game based mainly on physical strength to a more tactical and strategic approach. In addition to physical ability, planning, data analysis, real-time decision making and the ability to adapt during the game have become key elements for a team's success.

43

The presence of rugby in schools

Rugby is often an integral part of school sports programs in many parts of the world. It's a way to teach young people the importance of discipline, respect, and team collaboration. Schools offer young people the opportunity to develop their rugby skills, not only as athletes, but also as responsible and respectful individuals.

44

Impact of rugby around the world

As well as being a popular sport, rugby has a significant impact on the global landscape. Events like la Rugby World Cup not only promote sporting competitiveness, but also unity between different nations and cultures. Rugby unites people through a passion for sport, conveying a sense of belonging and promoting the spirit of fair play and solidarity around the world.

45

The tradition of numbered jerseys in rugby

In rugby, numbered jerseys play an important role in identifying and organizing players according to their positions on the field. Each number corresponds to a specific role: for example, number 1 is generally assigned to the left prop, number 9 to the scrumhalf and number 15 to the fullback. This system facilitates tactical communication between team members and allows referees and spectators to quickly identify each player's role during the game.

46

The art of the "lineout"

The "lineout" is a particular phase of the game that occurs when the ball leaves the side field. In this situation, the players of the two teams line up along the sideline and one player throws the ball into the center of the formation. This strategic moment allows teams to try to recover the ball through a coordinated jump of one or more players, offering the opportunity to regain possession of the ball and initiate offensive actions.

The tactical aspect of the "scrum"

The 'scrum' is one of the most physically demanding and technically complex situations in rugby. During a "scrum", eight players from each team meet head-on with the goal of gaining possession of the ball.

It is essential for players to maintain a stable position and apply coordinated pressure to try to push the opponent and win the ball. This tactical moment can significantly influence the outcome of the match.

48

The diversity of roles in rugby sevens

Seven-a-side rugby is a variant of 15-player rugby, but with a team made up of only seven players. This version of the game features a faster and more dynamic style, requiring players to have greater speed, agility, and ability to manage open spaces. Rugby 7s is played internationally in tournaments such as the Olympics, helping to promote and spread the sport to new regions and communities.

49

The role of video assistant referees (TMOs) in high-level matches

In high-level matches, the referee is assisted by the TMO (Television Match Official), an additional referee who uses video footage to support crucial decisions. The TMO is called upon to intervene in situations such as the validity of a try, potential fouls or dubious situations not perceived by the main referee. This system aims to ensure more accurate decisions and reduce referee errors during the game.

The importance of specific roles in rugby

Every field position in rugby plays a crucial role in determining the outcome of the match. For example, the hooker in a scrum is responsible for receiving the ball, while the hooker in touch is responsible for throwing the ball accurately during a 'lineout'.

The fly-half leads the attack and makes strategic decisions, while the full-back takes care of defence and counter-attacking opportunities. Each role requires specific skills, adaptability, and tactical vision, thus contributing to the dynamics of the game and the team's strategy.

51

Technology in modern rugby

Modern rugby has embraced technology to improve the quality of the game. From the use of the Television Match Official (TMO) system for contested decisions to the GPS technology worn by players to monitor performance and workloads, technological innovation has helped improve officiating, athlete training and in-depth understanding of the game .

52

The dynamics of rivalries in rugby

Rugby is full of historic rivalries between national teams and clubs, some of which have deep roots in tradition and history. For example, the derby between England and Wales is one of the most intense and exciting clashes in international rugby, characterized by fierce competition and a huge rivalry between the two nations.

These rivalries not only ignite the passion of fans, but often influence the flow and intensity of matches.

53

The social impact of rugby

In addition to its sporting aspects, rugby plays a significant role in promoting social integration and community engagement. Many teams and organizations use sport as a tool to address social issues, including inclusion projects for disadvantaged youth, education programs on health and the importance of physical exercise, as well as initiatives to raise awareness of diversity and inclusion.

54

The importance of physical preparation in modern rugby

Rugby is a sport that requires complete physical preparation. The workouts are designed to develop strength, endurance, agility, and speed, as well as focusing on the mental aspect of the athlete.

Coaches work on players' adaptability, preparing them to face a wide range of game situations. Nutrition and post-training recovery are equally important, with specific programs to ensure players are in optimal condition for matches.

55

The commitment of rugby teams in the community

Rugby teams often engage actively in the community, in addition to their on-field involvement. They organize charity events, participate in educational programs in schools, carry out voluntary work and promote social initiatives. This commitment represents an opportunity for rugby teams to contribute meaningfully to local communities, inspiring and supporting positive change.

The history of the introduction of women's rugby

Women's rugby has a rich and fascinating history, with the first documented matches dating back to the late 19th century. However, the official recognition and development of women's rugby in many nations has only occurred more recently. The increase in interest in the sport has led to greater visibility, promoting equality of opportunity, and enabling women to excel and contribute to the world of rugby.

57

The tradition of international tours

International tours are a significant part of rugby culture. National teams often undertake trips abroad to play a series of matches against other nations.

These tours not only provide competition opportunities, but promote knowledge sharing and interaction between different cultures, helping to build bonds and relationships within the global rugby community.

58

The inclusion of players from different sports disciplines

Many rugby players began their careers in different sports. For example, some successful athletes have had a background in football, track, and field, or even wrestling. This demonstrates the versatility of athletes in moving from one sport to another, bringing specific skills that enrich rugby and help create a variety of playing styles.

The origin of the term "Try" in rugby

The term "try" in rugby, used to indicate the scoring of a try, has curious origins, and does not derive from the English verb "to try". Initially, in the 19th century, when rugby was developing its rules, no direct score was awarded to score a try.

If a player managed to 'try at goal', they had the option of attempting the kick to get a 'goal'. Subsequently, the phrase "try at goal" was shortened to "try", and has remained an essential part of rugby parlance ever since.

60

The influence of scrum halves in controlling the game

Scrum-halves in rugby play a crucial role in controlling the game and organizing attacking actions. The scrum half acts as the team's main playmaker, coordinating attacks, making tactical decisions, and distributing the ball to other players on the pitch. Their ability to read the game, make quick decisions and coordinate the attack is crucial to the team's success.

61

The evolution of uniforms in rugby

Rugby uniforms have undergone a significant evolution over the years. From the early days when players wore relatively simple jerseys and shorts, uniforms have evolved into technical fabrics that offer comfort, breathability and durability.

Modern uniforms are also designed to withstand the physical stresses of the game, while maintaining a design that represents the teams' identity and heritage.

The impact of rugby in youth education

Rugby is often used as an educational tool in schools and communities to teach values such as respect, fair play, and teamwork. Rugby programs in schools promote not only physical activity, but also the formation of social and personal skills.

The experience of playing rugby at a young age offers boys and girls the opportunity to develop transferable skills, such as leadership and stress management, as well as encouraging a healthy lifestyle.

63

The importance of managing pressure at crucial moments

Rugby is a sport that tests athletes' ability to handle pressure during critical moments. The final minutes of a match, especially if the score is in the balance, require composure, concentration, and quick decisions. The ability to remain calm under pressure is essential to making decisive plays and making strategic decisions that can determine the outcome of the match.

The growth of rugby in Italy

In Italy, rugby has had constant growth in recent decades, becoming an increasingly popular sport. Although football remains the main sport, rugby has gained ground, especially in the Northern regions, where it has stronger historical roots.

Italy participates in the Six Nations tournament, a prestigious competition, and its presence has helped promote rugby in the country, increasing interest and participation at youth and amateur level.

65

The evolution of European rugby and club competitions

European rugby has seen the evolution of club competitions, such as the European Rugby Champions Cup and la European Rugby Challenge Cup. These competitions bring together the best clubs from different European nations, offering high-level entertainment and competition.

These tournaments have become a proving ground for the best talent and a showcase for diversity and competition in the European rugby landscape.

The rise of women's rugby in Europe

In women's rugby, Europe has also seen notable growth. National teams such as England, France and Ireland have established themselves as globally competitive teams. Competitions such as the Women's Six Nations and la Rugby World Women's Cup have helped promote the visibility and participation of women in rugby, stimulating ever-increasing interest in the sport among young female athletes across Europe.

67

The role of training schools in European rugby

Rugby training schools and academies in Europe play a vital role in developing young talent. These institutions offer an environment dedicated to technical and tactical training, as well as encouraging the personal and social growth of athletes.

Many of European rugby's emerging stars began their journey through these training schools, highlighting the importance of investing in the growth and development of promising young players.

68

The influence of different cultures in European rugby

European rugby is distinguished by the influence of the different cultures and traditions present in various countries. Each nation has its own peculiarities in the way of playing, in the playing styles and in the tactics adopted. The interaction between these cultures helps to make European rugby a fertile ground for diversity and innovation, offering unique and stimulating insights into the world of this sport.

69

The records of the longest rugby match

One of the longest rugby matches in history took place in 2015 in South Africa, between the High School and Polytechnic High School teams. The match, played to commemorate the school's centenary, lasted for 28 consecutive hours, setting a world record recognized by the Guinness Book of Records.

During the match, 60 hours of actual gameplay were played, with short breaks given to players to rest and eat.

70

The fastest try in the history of international rugby

The fastest try recorded in the history of international rugby was scored by Bryan Habana, a South African player, during the la Rugby World2007 Cup against England. Habana scored a spectacular try just 8.11 seconds into the match, outpacing the English defenders and reaching the in-goal in lightning-quick fashion, setting a record that still remains unbeaten.

71

The record of points scored by a single player in a rugby match

The world record for points scored by a single player in a 15-a-side rugby match belongs to Gareth Rees, a Canadian player, during la Rugby World Cup 1995. Rees scored a total of 30 points (two tries, four free kicks and two conversions) against team from Hong Kong, setting a record that still remains one of the most impressive in the history of international rugby competitions.

72

The largest victory in an international rugby match

The largest victory recorded in an international rugby match belongs to New Zealand, who defeated 1995 Tahiti with a final score of 145-17. This extraordinary victory by the New Zealand team remains one of the most stunning results in the history of international rugby.

73

Oldest player to make his international rugby debut

In 2007, Alejandro "Huevo" Di Nucci, an Argentine player, set the record as the oldest to debut in international rugby at 40. Di Nucci represented Argentina in the match against the Namibian national team during la Rugby World Cup of that year, proving that age is not always a limit in pursuing a passion for sport.

The birth of the rules of rugby

Rugby has its roots in British schools, mainly at Rugby School, where in 1823 a fundamental event in the history of the sport occurred: during a football match, a student named William Webb Ellis caught the ball in his hands and ran towards the opposing goal, giving life to a new game mode.

While the story is somewhat legendary, this moment is said to have inspired the first rules of rugby as a sport in its own right, which have evolved over the years.

75

The longest drop goal in rugby history

In the world of rugby, the drop goal represents one of the most spectacular and difficult plays to make. In 2013, during a French rugby match, Frederic Michalak, already an established player for the French national team, accomplished an extraordinary feat: he scored a drop goal from midfield. This incredible shot has been observed as one of the most memorable and extraordinary moments in the history of professional rugby.

Michalak demonstrated not only impeccable technique, but also extraordinary strength, kicking with precision and power from a remarkable distance, thus achieving an unprecedented result. The precision required for a drop goal is already remarkable, but the distance from which

76

The rivalry between Bath and Leicester rugby clubs

The rivalry between the English rugby clubs Bath and Leicester is one of the fiercest and longest in the history of English rugby. These two teams have a proud history and a history of significant success, competing at the highest levels of national and international competitions.

The matches between Bath and Leicester are not just sporting clashes but real spectacles that have generated epic and memorable moments in English rugby. This rivalry fuelled the passion of the fans, leading to matches full of tension and unpredictability, helping to define the history and very fabric of English rugby.

The first international rugby match

The event that marked the beginning of international rugby competitions was the first match between Scotland and England on 27 March 1871, held at Raeburn Place in Edinburgh. This historic match, considered rugby's first test match, represented a significant moment in the history of the sport. This pioneering match helped create rugby union and laid the foundations for future international competitions.

The teams represented two of rugby's pioneering nations and the match generated great interest, starting a tradition that would continue as rugby developed and expanded globally.

78

The role of third halves in rugby

In rugby values, there is significant importance placed on "third halves", the time after the match when teams meet to share a meal and socialise, regardless of the outcome of the match. This moment allows you to strengthen the friendship and respect between the teams, embodying the spirit of fair play and camaraderie that characterizes this sport.

79

The spread of rugby in the Pacific

Rugby has a strong presence and influence in Pacific nations, such as Fiji, Tonga, and Samoa. These nations have a long tradition in rugby, with a deep and rooted passion for the sport. Despite limited resources, these teams have managed to compete with the greatest rugby powers in the world, demonstrating innate talent, creativity in the game and impressive physical strength.

80

The history of the rivalry between New Zealand and South Africa

The rivalry between the New Zealand and South Africa national rugby teams is one of the most intense and historic in international rugby. These two teams have a history of epic matches and vibrant confrontations on the pitch. The rivalry was fuelled by memorable clashes that marked the history of rugby, creating matches of great intensity, spectacle, and sporting rivalry.

81

The phenomenon of "Galloping Greens"

The Australian club Randwick, known as the "Galloping Greens", has a rich history of success and influence in rugby. The club has produced some of Australian rugby's most legendary players, including several Wallabies, and has maintained a reputation for excellence and youth development over the years.

The evolution of tactics in modern rugby

Modern rugby has seen a significant evolution in playing tactics. From closed formations and purely physical play, we have moved on to more open and dynamic strategies. Teams now try to combine physical power with speed and creativity, trying to adapt to increasingly fluid and changing game situations.

The influence of rugby in cinema and popular culture

Rugby has left an indelible mark on popular culture and cinema. Films such as "Invictus" and "The Game of Their Lives" have told true and engaging stories linked to the world of rugby, highlighting the values of sacrifice, commitment and determination that characterize this sport.

These films have helped spread and promote the passion for rugby around the world, making the sport not only a part of the sporting world, but also of popular culture.

84

The "Sevens Rugby" phenomenon and the Olympics

Rugby Sevens is a faster and more dynamic version of rugby 15, with seven players per team instead of fifteen. This version of rugby has been included in the Summer Olympics since 2016, after decades of absence. The introduction of Rugby Sevens to the Olympics has helped expand the visibility of the sport globally, bringing a new energy and engagement to the Olympic movement.

85

The importance of "captain's runs" before matches

Captain's runs are light, strategic training sessions held the day before matches. These sessions mainly involve the team captain, who guides teammates through tactical and mental exercises, refining the final details for the upcoming match.

These sessions aim to focus the team, improve concentration, and define strategies to best face the opponent.

86

The culture of anthems before matches

Before rugby matches, teams often sing their national anthems or traditional songs, creating a moment of unity and national pride. This ritual helps create an emotionally charged atmosphere for both players and fans, representing a symbolic moment before entering the pitch.

The importance of injury management in rugby

Injury management is a crucial aspect in rugby, given the physical and contact nature of the sport. The teams have highly specialized medical teams and rigorous protocols to treat injuries and facilitate the recovery of athletes. Injury prevention is an important focus in training, while rehabilitation is key to enabling players to return to the pitch as soon as possible.

The role of managers and federations in rugby

Rugby unions and officials play a vital role in the development and organization of the sport. They deal with the regulation of competitions, youth development, management of rules and regulations, as well as the promotion of rugby nationally and internationally. Their commitment is crucial to ensuring the continued development of rugby in terms of quality, fairness, and growth around the world.

The Birth of British Rugby and Its Mythical Origins

The origin of rugby is steeped in legend, famously attributed to William Webb Ellis, a student at Rugby School in England. In 1823, he is said to have picked up the ball during a football game and run with it towards the opposition's goal line, thereby inventing rugby. Though this story is more myth than fact, it has become a foundational part of rugby's lore in Britain. The sport evolved rapidly in the UK during the 19th century, with the Rugby Football Union (RFU) being established in 1871. Since then, British rugby has significantly influenced the global development of the game, shaping its rules and playing style. This mythical beginning is not just a piece of folklore but has become a symbol of the innovation and uniqueness of the sport in Britain.

90

The Five Nations Tournament

The Five Nations, now the Six Nations with the addition of Italy in 2000, stands as one of the oldest and most prestigious rugby competitions in the world. Starting in 1883 as the Home Nations Championship among England, Scotland, Wales, and Ireland, it has become a staple in the international rugby calendar. British teams have played dominant roles in the history of the tournament, with England having the most total victories. The intense rivalries among these nations have produced some of the most thrilling and memorable matches in rugby history, showcasing the passion and skill inherent in British rugby.

91

The British and Irish Lions

The British and Irish Lions are a composite team drawn from the best players in England, Scotland, Wales, and Ireland. Formed every four years for a tour in one of the Southern Hemisphere rugby nations (New Zealand, Australia, or South Africa), the Lions' tradition dates back to 1888, making it one of the oldest and most prestigious teams in world rugby. The Lions tours are celebrated for their camaraderie and the intensity of the challenges, offering a unique opportunity for players from different nations to come together under a single banner. These tours not only showcase the skill and strength of British and Irish rugby but also promote unity and sportsmanship.

Evolution of Rules in British Rugby

British rugby has been instrumental in the evolution of the game's rules. The RFU, founded in 1871, was among the first organizations to codify rugby's rules. Over the years, these rules have been adapted to enhance the game, improve player safety, and make the sport more spectator friendly. For instance, the concept of the "forward pass" and rules around tackling have been refined over time to make the game more dynamic and safer. These rule changes reflect the continuous effort in British rugby to balance tradition with innovation, ensuring the game remains relevant and exciting.

Cultural Impact of British Rugby

Beyond the sporting aspect, rugby holds a deep cultural significance in the UK. It is regarded as a sport that fosters values like respect, loyalty, and bravery. British schools, in particular, have a long tradition of encouraging rugby as part of their educational ethos. Rugby also serves as a social gathering point, with local clubs acting as community hubs. Major matches, like those in the Six Nations, are national events that bring people together across team allegiances. The sport's ability to unite people, still values, and provide a sense of community underscores the profound cultural impact rugby has in Britain.

94

The Women's Rugby Revolution in Britain

The growth of women's rugby in Britain has been a remarkable aspect of the sport's evolution. The first recorded women's rugby match in Britain dates back to 1881, but it wasn't until the late 20th century that the women's game began to gain significant traction. The establishment of the Women's Rugby Football Union in 1983 marked a turning point, leading to more organized and competitive women's rugby across Britain. The England Women's Rugby team, also known as the Red Roses, has been particularly successful, winning multiple Six Nations Championships and performing strongly in the Women's Rugby World Cup. This rise in women's rugby has not only increased participation and interest in the sport among women but has also played a crucial role in challenging gender stereotypes and promoting equality in sports.

95

The Influence of British Rugby on Global Rugby Codes

British rugby has profoundly influenced various global rugby codes. Notably, the split between rugby union and rugby league in 1895, originating in Northern England, led to the creation of rugby league, a distinctly different code of rugby. This split was primarily due to disagreements over payment to players, with rugby league becoming a professional sport much earlier than rugby union. The influence of British rugby extends beyond these two codes, with British expatriates and military personnel historically helping to spread the game to countries like Argentina, Japan, and the United States, shaping the development of rugby worldwide.

96

Iconic British Rugby Stadiums

The stadiums where rugby is played in Britain are not just sporting venues; they are temples of history and passion. Twickenham Stadium in London, known as the "Home of England Rugby," is the largest dedicated rugby union venue in the world and has hosted some of the most significant matches in rugby history. Murrayfield Stadium in Edinburgh and the Principality Stadium (formerly Millennium Stadium) in Cardiff are other iconic venues, each with its unique atmosphere and history. These stadiums are more than just places to play rugby; they are cultural landmarks that have witnessed countless historic moments in British rugby.

97

The Amateur Ethos and Its Lasting Impact

The strong tradition of amateurism in British rugby had a lasting impact on the sport. For many years, rugby union in Britain remained staunchly amateur, with a strong ethos of playing for the love of the game rather than for financial gain. This principle shaped the culture of rugby, emphasizing values such as teamwork, sportsmanship, and integrity. The transition to professionalism in the mid-1990s was a significant change, bringing new challenges and opportunities. However, the amateur ethos continues to influence British rugby at the grassroots level, where the spirit of community and passion for the game remain strong.

98

Rugby and British Educational Institutions

Rugby has a long and storied connection with British educational institutions. Many of the earliest forms of rugby were developed and refined in British public schools and universities, with each institution often having its own version of the rules. This close association with education has given rugby a unique status in Britain. It's not just a sport but a part of the educational and cultural fabric. Schools like Rugby School, where the sport supposedly originated, and universities such as Oxford and Cambridge, with their annual Varsity Match, continue to play a crucial role in promoting and developing rugby talent and maintaining the sport's traditions and values.

The development of women's rugby globally
Over the past few decades, women's rugby has experienced significant growth globally. Sports federations and organizations have invested in the promotion and development of women's rugby, enabling women to play at all levels.

The inclusion of women's rugby in events such as the Rugby World Women's Cup has helped improve its visibility and accessibility, opening up opportunities for talented female athletes around the world.

100

The "Chalk Kicker" tradition in New Zealand rugby

In New Zealand, there is a unique rugby tradition known as the "Chalk Player". This tradition originates from a very particular superstition. Before an important match, a player on the team applies chalk to his hands and, sometimes, his legs or other parts of his body. The idea is that the chalk brings good luck and protects the player from injury during the match.

The players support each other by applying chalk and sharing some sort of symbolic connection before the game. This curious tradition demonstrates how deeply rooted beliefs and superstitions are in the world of sport, even in a physical sport like rugby.

Printed in Great Britain
by Amazon